DAMN THE PAIN
(LOVE, LIFE, AND LORD)

Subject Matter

DARRYL A. LEWIS

Damn the Pain
(Love, Life, and Lord)

Still Waters Publishing
Dam the Pain! (Love, Life, and Lord)

Published by Still Waters Publishing First Printed 2022

ISBN: 978-0-6927-8949-0

Printed in the United States of America

If thou canst believe
all things are possible
to him, that believes it.
Mark 9:23
Our doubts are traitors
and make us lose the good
we oft might win by fearing to attempt.
William Shakespeare

Dedicated to my mother, Mary (Ma) Frances Lewis,
my grandmother, Mary (Nanny) Elizabeth Craig
and my mother, Marie Camille Cooper

*I'll never be able to repay the tears, prayers, and reprimands by
way of backhand.
I love you!*

Table of Contents

CHAPTER ONE
LOVE

1. DAMN THE PAIN!
Remix with "It's a Man's World" by James Brown

Verse 1 (Piano + Drum + Bass)

So many days, I made you cry
I watched the pain roll down your eyes
Teardrops on your pillow
Like tattoos below your eyes
To validate the days and nights, and nights and days
You tried to question why!
I wish I had the answer!
I wished that I could change
I heard a voice whisper; it said
"Damn, damn the pain!"

Chorus 1 (Piano + Drum + Bass + Organ)

Damn my loneliness
Damn your sweet caress
Damn the reason, I wake up screaming out your name
I know I don't deserve you
But I need you just the same
As I drown in my own poison
I just, "Damn, damn the pain!"

Verse 2 (Piano + Drum [Steel hammer + Bass + Strings])

So many nights, I left you alone
You fell asleep, just staring, at your phone
While in the arms of a stranger
Exchanging words, we could never own
Our lips could taste the lies, I wondered why
When I had you there at home!
I went to the wishing well
And wished that I could change
My reflection looked back, and all it said was
"Damn, damn the pain!"

Chorus 2 (Piano + Drum + Bass + Strings + Organ + Background Vocals)

Damn my indiscretions
Damn my obsessions
Damn my reflections, for reminding me, who's the blame
I know I don't deserve you
But I needed you just the same
As I drown in my own poison
to just, "Damn, damn the pain!"

Change... +1 Step (Piano + Drum + Bass + Strings + Organ + Background Vocals)

Verse 3 Acappella (Extended)

Lord, they say that I'm a sinner
And I don't deserve Your ear
But I read somewhere that You were a forgiver
So, if You should take the time, hear!
Just send her back, and I promise I will change
I waited for Him to whisper
I prayed for Him to whisper
I heard the Lord whisper; He said
"Damn, damn the pain!"

Vamp Out...

Damn my indiscretions!
Damn my obsessions!
Damn my reflections!
Damn my loneliness!

2. MAY I BUY YOU A DRINK?

I'm hungry for your breast
like you gave birth to me.
The thought of you holding hands with another brings
out the worst in me.

I've tripped before but not this hard;
this is a first for me.
I thought about you 24/7 before I even met you
you, you are a voodoo curse to me.

The song of our bodies coming together
now that would be a heavenly verse for me.
Before I'd ever leave you
there would have to be
a funeral-home hearse for me.

As if you were an O.G. and
I was your foot soldier on the block
I would gladly put in work for thee.

The water from your oasis is the only thing that could
satisfy this thirst for me.
I'm talking a diamond
on your ring finger while on one knee.
It's for better or worse for me.

I would never lie or deceive you;
You are Goddess!
That would be blasphemy.

This whole thing is making my head spin
I'm losing my equilibrium
It's moving too fast for me!

Let me just slow this thing down!
Hello, may I buy you a drink?

3. MY POTENTIAL QUEEN
(You're Not Quite Ready)

I see you.
My perfect specimen of
sculptured flesh,
angelic smile fallen from rays of sunlight,
lips moist like virgin blades of grass
glistening from 5 a.m. morning dew
attempting to skew my sense of logic.

It's not that I don't want to.
Any man, woman, or beast
that falls prey to your siren-like stare
would crash their Greek vessel
in order to adore you but,
I am Nubian, in search of my queen,
and right now, you're not quite ready for what I do.

You're looking for a brother with arched eyebrows
and prettier than you.
You're looking for a brother with his pants sagging
showing more booty than you.

When you're making love
he's looking at himself in the mirror.
He's not even focused on you.
You're just a prop in the scene
to make him look good.
He's not even focused on you!

That food he's trying to feed you
ain't even good enough to make a good number two.
I'll make you a home-cooked meal,
massage your feet,
stimulate your pressure points,
and crack your toes!

That's right.
If you're my woman, I'm supposed to spoil you.

You're not quite ready
for a brother to put you on a pedestal
and coronate you as his queen.
You are looking for that "sexy brother"
that puts bros before hoes
And walks all over your self-esteem.

He's so selfish and insecure,
he destroys all your hopes and all your dreams.
He sees himself as an individual high scorer.
He couldn't imagine you as the MVP
on his championship team.

Do you really think that's sexy
when he disrespects you in front of the world
and feels it's okay to treat you mean?

Oh, my sister, my potential queen.

You need to look in the mirror and
acknowledge the fact
that you're made in God's image too!

You need a man that appreciates your very essence
and only puts God Himself above you.
He leaves little notes throughout the house
and in your purse that say,
"Baby, just wanted to remind you
that I love you!"

Oh, I understand.
You're still going through emotional rehabilitation
due to stunted growth
from negative baggage of the past
and you know it's true.

Darryl A. Lewis

A couple of dudes did you dirty
and now, you figure that's what dudes do.

   Your female is gift.
   Empty boxes are soon smashed.
   Pink ribbons and bows.

Now just marinate on that Haiku.

Your naïveté sheepishly reveals itself to me.
Your innocence touches the humanity in me.
Falling prey to our primal urges
is what brings about all this insanity that we see.
I unselfishly concede,
don't reach out for them but reach into you.
You don't get a pass
just because you have a nice...

You can call me twenty-four-seven
my ear is always here for you,
but right now,

you're not quite ready for what I do.

4. THE SAME BOTTLE
Intro—Drum

Verse 1 — (Drum, Bass)

There goes my illness and cure
with that devilish grin.
Behind those soft, glossy lips
is where my story begins.
I hate when she leaves.
Love to watch her walk away.
Before she goes through that door
I know I'll beg her to stay.

Pre-Chorus:

Oh, no, Doctor! — (70s organ)
You're mistaken for sure.
She can't be my illness
and then be my cure.

Chorus:

I thought she'd be heaven but sometimes she's hell.
I really don't know if she makes me better or well.
It's from the same bottle; I just can't tell.
It's from the same bottle
the same bottle
the same.

Verse 2:

Oh, how she makes me tingle
like cocaine in my veins.
I feel so confused
I think I'm going insane.
My mind tries to leave
wants to jump from this train.
Oh, one sip from her bottle, and

everything changes.

Pre-Chorus:

Oh, no, Doctor! — [70's organ]
You're mistaken for sure.
She can't be my illness
and then be my cure.

Chorus:

I thought she'd be heaven but sometimes she's hell.
I really don't know, if she, makes me better or well.
It's from the same bottle; I just can't tell.
It's from the same bottle
the same bottle
the same...

Bridge: (Spoken Word)

Pre-Chorus:

Oh, no, Doctor! — [70's organ]
You're mistaken for sure.
She can't be my illness
and then be my cure.

Chorus:

I thought she'd be heaven but sometimes she's hell.
I really don't know, if she, makes me better or well.
It's from the same bottle; I just can't tell.
It's from the same bottle.

5. THE SAME BOTTLE

I'm hooked on her smile and laughter; now that's dope.
Will I ever find a need for another? That's, nope!
My love isn't blind, Ray Charles, Stevie Wonder.
I have a full view of her seasons,
and I embrace her thunder.

I'll put a ring on her finger not one but, ten times,
So, when she raises her hands to the heavens,
the stars know that she's mine (2x)

I'm passionate about how I feel,
similar to "The Christ."
I melt when I'm in her embrace,
as if flames were embracing ice.

Then I boil and rise up to the clouds
that hold up the heavens.
Rain back down in the form of tears and precipitation
looking forward to becoming
the water for her irrigation
from my old-school, Mighty Clouds of Joy.
I'm uninhibited like a brand-new baby boy.
I can't take my eyes off of my favorite toy!

The seconds, the minutes, the hours,
the days continue to roll by but,
I have a primal infatuation with
the shape and the curvature of her bottle,
so, for me, it's but a blink of an eye.

Her opening is so inviting.
I anticipate it caressing my lips.
I place my palm on the nape of her neck,
slide down her side
past her waist and rest on the arch of her hip
pull her closer, to take a sip.
But wait!

Darryl A. Lewis

Her drink sometimes seems to poison me.
I'm intoxicated by this dichotomy
that keeps confusing me.
Should I have my lips to pull away, cease to quench?
Pray to God for self-restraint, with fist clenched.

Should I have my eyes turn away and escape her gaze
as it reaches the pit of my soul?
Like a wild-blue Pit Bull, it grabs hold.

Or should I grab my bottle and toss it into the wall
watch it shatter into a thousand pieces
and count the pieces as they fall?
I dare say, no, never, not at all.

For as the poison would spill,
my cure,
my remedy,
my joy would surely follow
because they are but one and the same
from the same bottle...

6. I NEVER TOLD YOU - SPOKEN

Hey, girl, is that you?
I haven't seen you in a long time.
As a matter of fact,
 I don't even remember you being this fine.

Oh, 'cause you're happy now?
At least I see you still got jokes.
Well, I'm happy for you.
I hope you didn't take offense to my little poke.

Yea, I put on a little weight.
No, it's cool; you're not being mean.
I understand now
why you used to make me eat all my greens.

I do have to say,
I missed all those home-cooked meals
Those walks at night, holding hands,
you trying to share how you feel.
Yet, I never told you

I never told you the things
that were really going on inside my head.
I played that macho role,
the *Man of Steel*,
like I didn't give a F@#%K instead.

I didn't know
or maybe I chose not to realize
That even if Superman falls the wrong way
He too can become emotionally paralyzed.

When in reality I was a little boy,
trapped inside steel and stone.
You could hear that little boy crying out.
You couldn't bear
to leave that little boy there alone.

You scratched and clawed to reach him.
You wore down your manicured nails,
blood coming from your fingertips.
You cried at night for him but to no avail.

Your friends never liked me.
They tried to convince you
that you deserved better.
Your best friend Felicia snitched,
said she saw some other female
wearing my birthday sweater.

My friends, weren't much help
other than getting high and flexing,
They said,
"If she starts tripping
buy her some flowers and chocolates;
double up on the sexing."

In my heart, I knew what you wanted.
You just wanted me to be me.
You were the best thing in my life.
I was too blind to see.
Yet, I never told you

I never told you how
My heart would try to see
through the spaces of the fingers of my ego.
My ego would whisper lies in my ear
to maintain control,
just wouldn't let me go.

I *should* have given,
but we can't relive the past.
Go ahead now to your,
Happily Ever After.
This kiss on the cheek
is but a farewell,
for an unfulfilled love,
behind the face of a fallen mask
I never told you...

7. I NEVER TOLD YOU
(Sample: "How Can You Mend a Broken Heart" by Al Green)

Verse 1

I never told you
That when you touched me
My spirit trembled like a leaf but...
My ego whispered, in disbelief
"Don't let them know you."
"What if they hurt you?"
"What will you do?"

Verse 2

I never told you
That when I held you
It sent warmth all over me
That in my eyes we both can see
I should have given
Life ain't worth living
Without you

Change:

How could I give so much without denying myself?
And why should I want to?
I wish I knew

Verse 3

I never told you
How much I need you
The way a tree must have the sun
Forever reaching to be one
Oh, how I need you
I live and breathe you
Yet I never told you

Verse 4

I never told you
That when you left me
You took my world and all my dreams
And left my pride for what it means
Pride can't make me happy
Reality, slap me
I'm the fool

Change:

How could I give so much without denying myself?
And why should I want to?
I wish I knew

Verse 5

I never told you!
How much I need you
I long to hold you!
I live and breathe you
I should have given
Life ain't worth living, without you...

8. I'M NOT GOING TO LOVE YOU UNTIL

No, woman
I'm not going to love you
until you've given me what I want.
I'm not going to love you
until you've given me
what physically and emotionally belongs to you.

I'm not going to love you
until you've satisfied my primal, instinctive inner dog,
whether sincere, convinced, coerced, or
I just happened to catch you
in a bad emotional state of mind.

I'm not going to love you until
you've repaid whatever minuscule favor I've performed
for you by some means of sexual gratification.
"What'chu going to do for me?!"

I'm not going to love you
until you've given me some of "that"!

Naïveté does not become you.
You know what I'm talking about.
I'm not going to love you
until I can beat my chest like a gorilla and say
"Yes, I've been there
I've had some of 'that'!"
Don't worry; I don't want to keep it.
I only want to use it until I am bored
and then I'll go and find another
to temporally medicate my own pain and emptiness.

No, woman
I'm not going to love you until...
I'm not going to love you until...

I'm going to love you

for the mere fact that you are a woman
a blessing on this planet.
I'm not saying this as a mere come-up or
because I'm "thirsty"
I say this because it is true.

God so loved the world
He gave His only begotten son but
God so loved mankind He made you, woman.
The physical manifestation of beauty.
The uniqueness that is you.
The diversity that is you.
The softness that is you.
The strength that is you.

Every time I think that I've discovered,
within my own limited scope
what I believe to be
the epitome of female beauty

you trick me.
You fool me.
You educate me.

You show me another example of female beauty
on the complete opposite side of the spectrum.

Woman, I've come to discover,
Your beauty is not merely defined by your age.
It's not merely defined by your shade or your color.

Not by the length or the texture of your hair.
It's not merely defined by
what you've got going on "down there."

Your beauty is not merely defined by
your shape or your size,
not merely by your calves or your thighs.
It doesn't even really matter

whether or not you have those bedroom eyes.

And I don't care if
you've been convinced by those other lies.
Woman, your beauty
is not necessarily defined by your booty
or lack thereof.

Woman, you are beautiful just because you are.

I love you for your embrace;
when you've invited me into your bubble,
into your holy space
with open arms.
I know that I'm blessed to be there.
Your space is sacred.

Without you,
I am no more than a lonely nomad
wandering in a land of lies and disappointments,
squeezing the juice from unequally yoked substitutes
to satisfy my carnal cravings and
discarding their empty carcasses.

With you,
I am more *me* than I could ever imagine.
Your reassuring smile is North Star
that jump-starts my journey to infinite possibilities!

Are you my Eve?
My missing rib?
My better half?
No, you are the completed whole
that complements my completed whole!
Together our vision is so clear I can smell it
like I can smell Big Momma's sizzling bacon
on a black cast-iron skillet on Sunday morning!
We quench our thirst with the sweet, fruity nectar of
fruition!

No, woman,
I'm not going to love you until
day becomes night, until wrong becomes right,
until the sun and all the stars cease to emit light,
until the children of Ishmael and Isaac come to an
agreement and cease to fight!
Woman, I'm just going to love you because
within the construct of my very being
I know that it's right.
No, woman,
I'm not going to love you until.
I'm not going to love you until.

I'm just going to love you.

9. I'LL TRADE A TEAR FOR A SMILE

Our friends, say they saw you with another man
At our favorite restaurant holding hands.
The thing that seems so hard for them to understand
is that it doesn't matter.

It doesn't matter;
no, I wouldn't care.
Even if they had recorded on their iPhone,
posted it on Facebook and YouTube,
had CSI verify the DNA with a lock of your hair.

That's three kinds of pain I would be willing to bear.

Your one moment of joy justifies those three kinds of
pain.
Expectations of playing footsies
under a quilted comforter while it rains.

There you go with that smile
melting my disappointment away.
A smile, a tender touch that gently caresses my cheek,
causes me to cheat when I play

"She Loves Me, She Loves Me Not" with
white, frustrated daisies that attempt to tell the truth.
 I won't let them!

I'll trade a tear
for those sporadic moments again, again, and again...

Sometimes the line is blurred
where the pain stops, and the joy begins.
Lies cloaked in gloss and pillowy-soft lips,
velvety-smooth skin that seems to have no end,
rounded hips a perfect fit for my hands to grip
to pull you closer for me
take in your mind-altering nectar
of your "forget-me-nots."

My index finger gladly reaches below my eye
to withdraw from my account
to invest in your affection.

I'll still trade a tear for a smile from you.

10. I'LL TRADE A TEAR FOR A SMILE
(Sample: "Love and Happiness" by Al Green)

Verse 1

When we first met, it wasn't this way.
When you smiled, I should have walked away.
Your love turned cold. I don't understand.
'Cause I'll do anything, to be your man.

Chorus

I'll trade a tear, for a smile, from you.
I'll trade a tear, for a smile, from you.
I'll trade a tear, for a smile, from you.
I'll trade a tear, for a smile, from you.

Verse 2

Sometimes I wonder what goes through your mind,
what kind of game you're playing on my time.
Is this my future loving you—
crying tears just to get me through?

Chorus

Trade a tear, for a smile, from you?
I'll trade a tear, for a smile, from you.
I'll trade a tear, for a smile, from you.
I'll trade a tear, for a smile, from you.

Change – (Escalate)

I know a man is not supposed to cry,
But life without you is a pain I can't deny.
I tried so hard; I tried so hard not to react, but
why waste these tears, if they can't bring you back?

Chorus

Trade a tear, for a smile, from you?
I'll trade a tear, for a smile, from you. (3x)
(Oh, oh, oh, oh, oh, oh)
(Chorus in unison)
La, la, la, la, la... La, la, la, la, la... La, la, la, la, la

11. WHAT MAKES YOU DON'T CALL ME UP?

Verse 1

First time I saw you, dancing there in the park
I knew right then; I no longer owned my heart
(It belonged to you)
Rhythm in your blood and drumbeats in your flesh
Your inviting gyrations put my soul to the test

I asked your name; you silently touched my lip;
First with a finger but then you placed a kiss
The taste of heaven still lingers on my tongue
We danced and held each other, the whole night long

Chorus:

(4x) What makes you don't call me up?

Verse 2

We danced the passion dance under the blushing moon
Sleep uninvited, embraced our lover's swoon
I dreamed we held each other for 100 years
But when I woke up, a note described my fears

It said, "I loved the moment; let us preserve it in our hearts
We've tasted paradise; let's not let the flavor depart
We've had heaven, you and me, right here on Earth
Time can only change it, steal it with a curse!"

Chorus:

No, don't run away! Call me up!
What makes you don't call me up?
What makes you don't call me up?
What makes you don't call me up?

12. LOVE OR LUST (PART 1)

I am metaphysically,
and biologically attracted to you.
Though there are other Queens
and Goddesses in the room
with the same physical attributes as you,
my eyes may wander but
for some strange reason —
 I'm automatically and uncontrollably
drawn back to you.
Is this love or is this lust?

I don't subscribe to love at first sight.
I prefer to take that first bite.
Though that first taste may seem just right,
What dat aftertaste be like, at daylight?

When we look into each other's eyes
can we honestly say that our mutual attraction
is based upon the characteristics of love —
or have we fallen prey to the primal urges
that tend to draw a man and woman together
for the purpose of procreation?

Procreation — [Laughter]
that's a nice, clean, clinical way to put it
when in actuality,
procreating is the furthest thing from our minds.

I initially anticipate lust!
I anticipate you and I in a syncopated thrust!
I anticipate your soft lips attacking my mouth
attempting to suck the very soul from my body.
I look forward to swooping you up in my arms,
like a proud warrior
returning home from a battle with Babylon
in desperate need of his woman

to make him forget all the pain and death behind him.
I toss you upon a soft bed of red roses:
you fall in slow motion.

I predict clothes being ripped off,
thrown recklessly about the room.
I foresee you welcoming me
with those come-hither eyes,
open arms and open thighs.
A physiological reaction occurs,
that I have no control of when I just think of you.

Your pheromones travel throughout the room
like a dancing, erotic temptress spirit
rise up my nostrils,
to paint sensual masterpieces in my mind,
of you sweaty and glistening
as I massage and knead your muscles
with fragrant oils.

Your moans embrace me so tight
that I can barely breathe!

Your petals open freely,
entice me to taste their nectar.
Your tulips upon my two lips.
Please excuse me as I lick my fingers.
I dare not waste a sip.
Agave-like drops,
slide across taste buds, cause me to trip.

"You are my starship. Come take me up tonight..."

I have never tasted anything so sweet —
Even the bees envy me.

Moonlight reflections travel through windowpane,
twinkle upon your naked body.
Black shadows mimic our moves upon white walls
resembling some tribal, voodoo, mating, ritual dance.

Gyrations work themselves up
to a fever-pitched frenzy.

Heartbeats pounding like bass drums.
Flesh on flesh, bodies smashing
until nerve endings are numb.

"That's a headboard and a wall!
Where you gon' run?"
Thy kingdom comes!

We collapse — in a pool of our mutual contentment,
barely cognizant of our surroundings
gathering staggered gasps of air.
But I want to get to know *you.*
I have these tickets to Cancun or Jamaica
I was just wondering....

13. A FATHER'S CONFESSION

I love my daughter but,
I hate my daughter.
She changed the dynamics of
my entire game.
I love my daughter but,
I hate my daughter.
Since my daughter came into my life
I can't look at anyone's daughter the same.

It's so scary for me to think
that one day someone's son
will look at my daughter the same way I look at others.
Sometimes I just watch my beloved jewel
in her angelic slumber,
and hyperventilate as I recall
she's the result of how I one day looked at her mother!

Lord, please forgive me for all my, "Yo, yo's," and
"Hey, girl, you got a nice future behind you."
Any potential young suitors
that are within the sound of my voice!
If you ever say that to my daughter,
I pray lightning strikes you down and blinds you!

What penance must I perform
to be forgiven for my past evil deeds?
100 Hail Marys, 100 Our Fathers
while kneeling on raw kernels of dry rice,
spread on the concrete floor,
beneath my bloody knees?
I'll publicly
stand in front of the congregation and confess
as those ladies in the flock silently mouth,
"Snitch on yourself,
but don't mention my name, please!"

I'll recite the Buddhist mantra,

Nam-myoho-renge-kyo
in the woods, butt naked,
under a hive
while continuously being stung by bees.

I'll constantly repeat the 42 Admonitions of Ma'at
while building a life-size replica, of ancient Kemet
with toothpicks, sand, and goat cheese!

I'll be that Hotep
that sidesteps
any queen that lacks knowledge of self
and help her to overstand
it's not just about me getting in her draws.

I'll be that emotional punching bag
for any woman suffering through menopause.

Darryl A. Lewis

I'll do whatever it takes,
to erase any sins upon my wretched soul
regarding someone else's daughter in the past.
For any time, I merely lusted
for another father's daughter's flesh
And saw her just as another piece of ...

God, I know what You did;
I see Your plan to get my actions under control.

You said,
"I'll give you a beautiful daughter
that gives you her unconditional trust,
loves you with all her essence, her heart, and her soul.

Then you'll know how it feels,
when the moon is full,
and a young wolf comes knocking at your door
pants sagging and earring in his lip."

Yes, Lord, I have the love of Jesus in my heart, but
I still keep a gun, on my person
loaded with a full clip.

Once she was born,
I heard that voice from above again say,
"Thy life no longer belongs to thee!
A seed of revelation has been passed on to you;
this baby girl will show you
how unconditional true love should be."

As time went on,
I realized that I needed her,
just as much as she needed me.

I love my daughter.
I don't hate my daughter.
I'm a better man
and she's the blame.

My Pentecost,
upper-room experience
new way of thinking
holy spirit descended —
She has been my flame.

14. I KNOW YOU II / MANIFESTATION

My right arm
is awakened by a cool pillow.
I embrace it for your scent
only to realize an empty bed.

I'm relieved
 to find you sitting at the kitchen table
sipping herbal tea from your favorite cup.
The cup that you made in that class;
you were so proud.
That class that showed you everything tastes better
with pride.

You're listening to jazz,
reading Langston Hughes'
Ask Your Momma, smiling,
I'm just an "Invisible Man"
standing there at a distance.
I hesitate to disrupt
this portrait of beauty before me.

Your legs are folded
in the chair Indian style.
You have on those shorts I like,
a spaghetti-strap tee
that tastefully reveals your neck, upper back, and
shoulders;

shoulders that invite me to massage them, massage
away the tension and the stress.

The stress
that goes along
with just being a woman.

I slowly walk toward you.
You eventually see me approach.

You acknowledge me
with those eyes and
that same smile you have on that picture;

that picture you gave me
to put in my wallet
so, I would never forget you.

Did you know, your image,
your smile is tattooed in my brain?
I bring you with me wherever I go.
It's been there for an eternity.

I gently, but firmly, knead your back muscles.
Brush your shoulders with my lips;
kiss them the way they enjoy being kissed,
as that sensitive part of your *neck* looks on
jealously anticipating *its* turn.

I watch the goosebumps arrive in formation.
I feel your body slightly tremble.
My ear, close to your mouth,
hears a distinct slow moan.

You remove your earphones,
place your book on the table,
look deep into my eyes,
converse with my soul.

You gently place your palms on my face,
and kiss me softly
again, and again, and again
as if you were savoring the taste of my lips.

I feel the earth tremble.
We hear Erykah Badu in the background.

You wrap your arms around my neck
hug me strongly.
I lift you off the chair.

Darryl A. Lewis

You then wrap your legs around my waist;
we kiss even more passionately.

We've become one flesh.
I am you and you are me;
we are equally yoked;
our hearts beat in unison.

I feel you collapse in my arms
from the aerobics
of emotions, and contentment.

You nuzzle your head upon my chest.
I feel your breath on my skin.

Though I haven't *physically* met you.

I already know you.

15. I JUST WANNA BE

Chorus – [acapella]

I just wanna be all that you need
If you're short on blood, I'd freely bleed
If you can't draw air, my lungs I would gladly share
I just wanna be all that you need

Verse 1- [Drums: kick, closed-hh, rim]

Here I am
before God and man on bended knee
You who saw past my imperfections
and accepted me
Don't know what I did to deserve you but
Till my last breath, I'm going to serve you!

Chorus – [Piano, Drums]

Verse 2 – [Drums, Bass]

This ring I hold that wraps around our souls
shall never end
Words can't express my heart's true emotions
with sound or pen.
May I have your hand forever?
You and I eternally together.

Chorus – [Drums, Piano, Bass, Strings]

Bridge -

Oh, your softness changed me!
Oh, your strength complements me!
Your eyes, they see through me!

[Spoken Word]

Chorus [Full Chorus modulation one step]

I just wanna be all that you need
If you're short on blood, I'd freely bleed
If you can't draw air, my lungs I would gladly share
I just wanna be all that you need
I just wanna be all that you
be all that you

[1,2,3,4...]
[Come back Acappella, with loud hand claps]
[Vamp Out]

Spoken Word
I want every individual cell of my body
to take you in just short of the point of burst.
You are my cool, refreshing drink of water
in the middle of a burning desert.

When the morning sun
pushes the moon aside,
taps me on my shoulder,
I want to wake up to your smile.

I've put down my guards.
I unconditionally make myself vulnerable to you.
I know that there's no need to fear.
You are dreams, prayers, meditations, and fasting
manifested.

Our spirits are braided,
an unbreakable rope.
Two voices that gather on one accord.
God is in our midst.

I'm intoxicated by contentment.
It would take the energy of the sun,
a thousand tongues,
and an eternity to describe!

Know this like you know there was a yesterday!
Know this like you know that there is an above and
below!
Know this like you know you were born!
Here on one knee,
before God and man,
diamond in hand,
I humbly ask for your forever.
I just wanna be all that you need...

CHAPTER TWO
LIFE

1. WHAT IS YOUR COLOR?

We all have our unique, individual color
which contributes to this masterpiece
that we call the Universe.
So, when I wake,
I wipe the sleep from my eyes,
look in the mirror and ask myself

What is your color?

No, not that "What hood you from?
Who are you claiming?"
color.

No, not that "He be singing the blues" or
"He be be-bop flaming"
color.

No, not that "I'm half African and Cherokee on my
mother's side,
Spanish, Irish, French, and Italian on my father's side"
color.

No, not the obvious color that you mark for the Census
Bureau
so, the government can keep track of you
color.

No, not that "Hey, how did they get in front of you,
and they used to be in the back of you?"
color.
The question is
What is your color?

Not that "separates you from him or us from them"
color,

but that color that you embody

that was given to you
from the One Omnipotent Father
of whom there is no other
color.

That "Bring us all together
to complete one divine portrait,
we call the Infinite Universe"
color.

No, not that
"I hate that color for what it has done to *my* color
and every other color throughout time"
color.

Not that "eye for an eye" color
That "leaves two colors just standing there blind"
color.

Knowing I need their color to *be*
in order for my color to stand out and so vibrantly
shine
color.

Knowing that they have God in their color
just like I have God in mine
color.

Have you seen your color?
Do you know your color?
Maybe you've been frightened by your color?

Does your color sing?
Does your color dance?
Does your color paint?
Does your color write?
Does your color fight for other colors?
Does your color have visions
of magnificent monuments
not yet seen by anyone outside of your mind?
Does your color teach?
Does your color lead?
Does your color inspire other colors?

Embrace your color!
Nurture your color!
Proudly and boldly proclaim your color!
Not with mere words but with actions!

[Change: Preacher's Voice]
Imagine the one great Omnipotent God
has received a revelation of *the* most magnificent
portrait
that of which Renoir, Picasso, Jean-Michel Basquiat
could not begin to imagine in one thousand eternities
of all their dreams combined.

He is so overwhelmed by revelation, inspiration,
expectation.
He runs to the canvas and begins to paint.
As He raises His mighty arm,

angels and saints begin to jump up and down in unison
in anticipation of you and your color.

With every meticulous placement of each color,
with every stroke of His glorious paintbrush, the heavens begin to tremble,

the stars scream out,
"Yes!" in expectancy of
you and your color.
To complete His glorious creation!
The tip of the brush approaches the canvas and...

I am awakened every morning
by an omnipresent alarm clock
beating upon my skull like a concrete mallet,
asking that eternal question
What is your color?

2. ECCLESIASTIC 3

(Inspired by Gil Scott Heron)
He told me the revolution will not be televised!
He told me.
I took it for granted or
maybe I didn't quite understand it,
but he told me!

I just thought it was a cool thing to listen to.
I dug the cool talk, afros, and bell bottoms,
but oh no,
was he talking to me?

My complacency
has created a latency
between the reality, the actuality
of who I aspire to be.

Is it because
the black man now has the option
to sit in the front of the bus?
Is it because my dollars can be so *easily integrated*
with them
and such a challenge to be *segregated* with us?
No Tulsa, Oklahoma.
No Black Wall Street.
No possibility of "Us We Trust."

Is it because,
my generation has yet to witness *blackberry season*?
Chickadees swooping down
from top of the Big House,
"*Daddy-Whys?*"
manifest themselves as daddy's pride
rolls down daddy's eyes.
Babies holding daddy's *trembling* hand.
Daddy holding down his head, feeling less than a man.

Darryl A. Lewis

Blackberry bushes bought and paid for
lined up for acres outside of the back door.
Virgin berries plump and ready for the plucking.

Chickadee bird claws and beak stained,
dripping blackberry juices.
Mmm, so sweet (as he licks his fingers).

Or is it because my generation has yet
to feel the stinging slash
of an overseer's cat-o'-nines,

separating the skin from our backs
and our sweaty behinds?
Sweat rolling like 400 years,
400 years of Mamma's tears.

While I was focused on dipping,
"Cloud 9 tripping"
they just reshaped the whip into
white booty so fine.

Later on, they even offered me the crack.
I'll be damned
I even accepted that —
with a naive, gullible, unsuspecting mind.

Not just then but even today
I can't discount the message because even
"The Messenger" fell prey— to "Angel Dust."

"The Visionary,"
"Verbal Revolutionary,"
tried to tell me, to paraphrase.

The revolution will not be televised.
Dare it fall prey to entertainment's lies.
Watered down, edited, rearranged, and quantized
to be a more palatable package for the masses

and more abundantly commercialized
for profit!
Please, stop it!

Like Blues.
Like "Blue-Eyed Soul."
Like "Blue-Eyed Hip-Hop."
Like "Blue-Eyed Rock and Roll."

The revolution should be raw and butt-naked
a slave who has taken his last slash of the whip,
ripped from the bosom of his motherland
like suckling babe is ripped from his mammy's tit.

Hear the mother's cries fade off into the distance
as they bounce off hulls
of the large-bellied slave ships,
only to drown in dark, watery abyss.

Stripped of his name.
Stripped of his family.
Stripped of his native tongue.
Stripped of his humanity.
His nose pressed against the precipice of insanity.

On behalf of the Negro race,
I hereby second the motion
of Amiri Baraka's submission
of an injunction for the perpetrators of these atrocities
to cease and desist.

The *black man* will exist!
The *black man* will exist!
The *black race* will exist!

Hear the pop of the rope-band as it rips
from his wrist
what a twist.

With taut, glistening African muscles

Darryl A. Lewis

black man makes eye contact
with the perpetrator of this injustice.

With tribal lips he states,
"If I have to leave this earthly place
your hand will never again touch us.

I read yo' Bible and Ecclesiastic 3.
Like a beaming light from heaven
it was shining on me."

He looks past the perpetrator's eyes,
deep into his soul.
He sees a frail, pathetic image of a man
trembling, begging for mercy.

"Please," the perpetrator begs
while huddled in the fetal position,
"I know I will never be,
half the king that I see.
So, I cry out to the compassion and forgiveness
that's in your DNA
that you have shown again and again, and again,
throughout history.

Please, don't hurt me.
Senegambia, Mali, don't hurt me.
Kongo. Please don't hurt me!

In Jesus' name.
Turn the other cheek.

It's not these earthly riches that you seek.
Don't jeopardize your opportunity
to sit by the master's feet!

Way up yonder, there be mansions
streets of gold,
an opportunity to redeem your filthy souls.

Look, way up yonder!
Can't you see?
Right there, Elijah's Chariot!"
[GUNSHOT!]
[FADE TO BLACK]

3. I AM SUBJECT MATTER

I am more than a bag of shiny swag.
I am more than the smoke that dissipates
into the nothingness from a Londoner's fag.
I am more than gold bars in a Gucci bag,
I am Subject Matter!

I am more than insignificant spurts of air
in various intonations.
I am the micro-essence of "let there be...!"
and then there was creation.

I am the seed of thought
that feeds the belly of conscious starvation.
I am the twisted wire hanger
that aborts the lies of *The Birth of a Nation*.

I am Chocolate Thunder,
Shaq Diesel,
Vince Carter,
Monster Dunk
shattering the backboards of all this ignorance.

I am more than Flavian interpretations
and allegory on white pages.
I am Medu Neter
on caves and tomb walls from ancient sages.

Dead Sea Scrolls,
mysteries and revelations yet untold.
I am whisperings,
ancestors 'whisperings
that fall on bended ear,
spiritual locations of treasures and gold.

I am Big Momma's recipe for chicken soup

passed down by word of mouth from generation to generation
that heals the sick, pathetic soul.

I am griot,
town crier on mountaintop.
"Quick, quick, gather your belongings!
 Swing low, sweet chariot!"

I am vibrations
riding on hand clap, foot stomp, and choir!
Sly and the Family Stone's
"I Want to Take You Higher."

I am Billie Holiday's "Strange Fruit."
Nina Simone's "Mississippi Goddam."
Max Roach and Abbey Lincoln's "Triptych."
Marvin Gaye's "What's Going On?"
Celia Cruz's "La Vida Es Un Carnaval."
N.W.A.'s "Fuck the Police!"
Sam Cook's
"A Change Is Gonna Come" Oh, yes it will.
They can no longer justify taking another
black life at will.
I'm George Clinton's
"...the bigger the headache, the bigger the pill"—

I'm not taking this platform for granted
to merely entertain you.
Hopefully, I remain with you.
I am Subject Matter!

4. LIVES MATTER IN A FLORIDA CLUB

All lives do matter.
Human beings in Orlando on June 12, 2016,
their lives mattered.
There is no outside looking in, only looking within.
Tolerance, love, and peace are what matter.

All God's creations matter.
The Omnipotent God
who resides in our DNA.
Allahu Akbar
resides in all,
knows all,
creator of all,
is incapable of error.
Who am I to judge,
with my finite understanding, His creation?
My jihad is within myself.

Who am I to carry around a bag of stones,
verbal stones, subliminal stones, metal or brass stones,
to cast at images of Yahweh that I can't comprehend?
Am I so pure, am I so perfect, am I truly without sin?

My sword is dry
and has not been anointed with the oil of Jehovah
to be thrust in the navel of Gomorrah.
I prepare my slingshot for holy war
seeking to destroy the giant Philistine,
but in actuality, I am Goliath.

Bags of stones
are stored in my closet
alongside my skeletons.
Skeletons pushing against door hinges,
attempting to escape.

Skeletons peering through keyholes

and watching in awe of my hypocrisy.
The hypocrisy that insists on casting boulders
at my mirror images.

Mirrors sometimes crack,
but boulders roll downhill
And smash against my foot.

I scream out from the pain
that travels through my body;
I see blood as I fall
and seek someone else to blame for my suffering.

I lie there on the cold concrete sidewalk,
a pathetic, putrid pile of rubble
smelling of urine and sweat,
communing with giant cockroaches,
wallowing in my self-pity.

Sounds of footsteps and traffic pass me by.
With squinting eyes
and the tongue of a poisonous snake,
I randomly spit venom:
"You, over there,
how can you embrace
and hold swinging hands of contentment
amidst my pain?

You, over there,
how can you walk through me
as if I were a ghost, mock me with your laughter
and the details of your intimate conversation
amidst my grief?"

I focus on you!
I dare not focus on myself!
I dare not focus on myself!

That would force me to scrutinize my insecurities,
my lack,
my wretched shortcomings,
my unyielding search,
my loneliness.

The truth would be unbearable.
I damn you,
but in reality, I damn myself.
I create an ice sculpture of a martyr called "I"
that melts from the rays of reality,
and evaporates into insignificance.
All lives don't matter!
My life doesn't matter!
[GUNSHOT!]

5. THE WIZARD OF OZ!

All Lives Matter? Really?

Indigenous red lives
observed white immigrants
running bare and eating their babies due to starvation
when they arrived in the New World, Roanoke.
Red lives showed compassion
taught white lives how to exist and thrive, Jamestown.
Red lives jump-started our so-called manifest destiny!

To show their appreciation
White lies had blue lives to escort red lives
on a trail of tears,
and out of the goodness of their hearts,
blue lives gave red lives
blankets infected with smallpox to keep them warm.
White lives then
stole as much of a red lives' future as they could
by pretending to *be* red lives for five dollars
passed it down to the children of white lives.

Stop me when I'm lying

Four score and seven years ago
white forefathers, legislated, that black lives be
enslaved,
hunted down, beaten, sex trafficked and auctioned off,
families torn apart, never to be joined again.

No, this wasn't Hitler's Auschwitz death camps
nor Russian Gulags
nor Cambodian killing fields.
This occurred right here in the land of the free.

And by the way, Jim Crow never died;
it still hovers above the heads of black lives

pecking and pecking and pecking and pecking...

Stop me when I'm lying

There is a dissonance between
their constitutional-political-campaign rhetoric
and reality.

We hear them behind closed doors!

"Those red lives just won't die; put them on
reservations; drop them to their wounded knees!

Keep your boots on the necks of those black lives.
They make good ornaments
for the branches of strong trees!

Pink lives should be barefoot
and pregnant,
and in the kitchen.
Our numbers are decreasing!
We must control their wombs!
"Oh, say can you see!?"

"Those brown lives are taking our jobs;
separate them from their babies
and put them in cages!

The rainbow lives were properly categorized
in the DSM's pages!
If there isn't a bucket of gold coins at their feet,
rainbow lives should all burn in hell!"—

I'm getting discombobulated with all these thoughts
inside my head, of examples and samples;
I know I'm starting to ramble.
ADHD causes me to have flashes of the Preamble.

I see "We the people..."
but "We the people"

see "He's the people"
hiding behind Star-Spangled Banners
feverishly turning gears
to keep us divided and conquered.

No,
communism, capitalism, cannibalism are not the problem.
It's them:
The red, the white, and the blue!

6. JOHN BROWNS

Buckets of remorse spill from tear ducts,
roll down rosy cheeks,
pool into a Dead Sea.

Appalled,
you bombard the ears of your forefathers
until they turn in their graves,
from your question: "Why!?"
Cognizant of the atrocities
beyond the spoon-fed school curriculum
that can't be denied.

Even though Big Momma said,
"If she can't use my comb,
don't bring her home!"
Even though Grandpa said,
"Don't trust 'em
no farther than you can throw 'em!
Leave them, devils, alone!"
My ancestors had their reasons.
I hope you understand.

Even though the Bible
that they gave us said
"God punishes the children
for the sin of the parents
to the third and fourth generation,"
I won't cast that second stone.
As an innocent, young babe
you don't choose the skin that you own.

No, I don't fault you
I appreciate you, John Browns,
and your sons that die on my behalf.
I reach my hand out,
holding an olive branch earnestly in love,
in hopes that floods of fear, greed, selfishness, subside.
We can bask in the peace of mind
that any human being would dream.
The hue of our skin will be *socially* irrelevant one day
as the color of our hair or our eyes.

If we both came from the womb of our mother Lucy,
we should agree that we are one family
and abolish that pungent smell of *hate*
that we both despise.

Darryl A. Lewis

I don't forget *them*, my ancestors.
I am, due to their sacrifices.
I know that *you* are not *them*, your ancestors.
You have awakened from their darkness.
Your moral consciousness
overwhelms the birthright of your legacy.

Even though there are no number of reparations
that could right the wrong that was committed,

I don't fault you, John Browns.

7. BUTT NAEKITT

I *like* to see my poems Butt Naekitt at times,
they are the bodies of my women.
I *appreciate* my words spread out, plain and
vulnerable on white sheets
so, I can get all up in 'em.

I *love* my papyrus to give an illusion
that I'm the first to have been there.
Well-groomed, I massage it with the vocabulary of my
mind.
I close my eyes and have intercourse with the who,
what, why, when, and where.

Beyond ménage à trois, an orgy of adjectives,
I see, hear, taste, touch, and smell.
Closed eyes can't see thin lines,
fantasy or reality, at times it's hard to tell.

I always like the content to be inviting,
bedroom eyes, unclothed, in a position of surrender.
Acrobatics and soundtracks, like zippers and snaps,
sometimes get in the way and merely hinder.

From time to time, I like a challenge,
metaphors, puzzle pieces, and parables.
Put together like Bible-verse-allegories,
allusions In Intimate variables.

I'm not always trying to be
that "Queen's English" intellectual.
Yes, I know this would be the perfect place,
to own up to my perverted mind,
and insert the perfect rhyme, sexual
but I'm passionate about my words, my stanzas
and the elements of this piece are contextual.

Darryl A. Lewis

Wordplay
is the foreplay,
gets the juices of my brain flowing.
Expressions uninhibited, tell-tales are showing.
Poker faces, long gone,
excitement is the anticipation of not knowing.
Caught up in the faith of inspiration, that upper room
spirit flowing.

Melodic syncopations mimic a baby-making song.
Homonyms happily, humping, hip bones
Butt Naekitt, groans, and moans...

[Cell Phone Rings]

"Hello, I'll have to call you back!
Now's not the time for small talk on cell phones..."

I apologize for the interruption.
Please, permit me to continue on.

Begging, bare-back, bare-black on white horse,
body of work, flinch and jerk,
percolators on high, bubbles and perks
alliteration pouring out in rapid-fire.
Sweat glands attempt to alleviate the heat of my desire.

Gripping tabletop to the point of *cracking!*
Stage presence is *attacking!*
Beads of water rolling down the spine of my back.
We make spiritual contact!
Me and pen and paper have MUTUAL CLIMAX—

[Breathing]

I give myself finger snaps!
The words and I exit, embrace as we take a nap,
Butt Naekitt.

8. I DARE YOU!

I dare you to look in the mirror
and tell that person staring back at you
that you will no longer try and be *that* person you idolize or envy. From here on out, you're going to be the best you!

I dare you to stick out in the crowd and no longer walk lockstep with the status quo. To know that your voice, hands, and feet are the unique paintbrushes that paint exclusive colors that contribute to this masterpiece we call the universe!

I dare you *not* to smile, laugh, bow, curtsy, turn left or right, go forward or retreat on command, when it contradicts everything that you hold near and dear to your inner core, your very being!

I dare you to make a change;
your present lifestyle is deranged.
I dare you to take steps to help yourself.
The world needs *your* help!

Chorus:
I dare you!
I dare you!
I dare you!
I dare you!

Break: (Death Metal Vocal) 2 Bars:

I dare you to move forward or get the hell out the way because your fermentation in stagnation is nauseating and debilitating to the growth of a whole nation and a waste of the "Big Bang," which stimulated the creation!

I dare you to raise a flag that represents you in support of an entire conglomerate of individuals that represent themselves and a "whole entire" movement, even though "whole entire" is redundant.

I dare you to tear the cataract off of your eyes that prevents you from seeing the hypocrisy that surrounds you. To realize what surrounds you is not really your reality but a figment of your imagination, and that your inner choices and perspectives have the potential to project a reality of your choice!

I dare you to make a change; your present lifestyle is deranged. I dare you to take steps to help yourself. The world needs *your* help!

Chorus:
I dare you! (4x)

Break: (Death Metal Vocal) 2 Bars:

9. TELL MY STORY IN ONYX INK

She knocks on the wooden door of the upper room,
partners with the holy ghost,
spiritual flames land on her body
and she dances in tongues.

Her ink is onyx.
Her holy book is exquisitely soft leather-bound.
Though others may be drawn
by the calligraphy of her eyes,
they can't comprehend her message
because it's not meant for them to understand.
It's our story.

The sway of her hips writes a message in cursive
that was only meant for us to read.
Her hypnotic cadence
blocks out all exterior distractions.
I encouraged her with the power of my drums,
"Tell my story!"

The vibration of bass drum
places its palms
on the left and the right side of her hips
in preparation for a dance
below moonlights and fluorescent skies.
Her lips gently mouth,
"I will tell our story."

Her movements are parables.

To them,
knowledge of the mysteries
of the kingdom of heaven have not been granted.
Her eyes, shoulders, arms, hands, hips, legs, and feet
join together to create an intricate sign language.
My carnal desires are secondary right now.

"Just tell my story."

I encourage her with the sincere heart of my Sangban.
The superlatives, adjectives,
and adverbs of my Kenkeni
cosign, empathize, improvise, and synchronize
with the movements of her body.
My Djembe communicates with her leaps
"Tell my story!"

The intensity of her movement increases.
Her ebony glistens
reflects the twinkle from the eye of the sun.
Her panacea glides through the air
rests on my lips: it tastes like home.

Darryl A. Lewis

The beginning and end of each phrase,
the change of subject
her body springs, her arms reach to heaven,
angels toss another letter for her to catch
with her outstretched fingertips.
Her feminine captures my attention.
The movement of her African cloth
embellishes each phrase
as it sends sweet pheromones
wafted by her pirouette to my imagination.
"Tell my story!"

If those who attempted to end *my story*
by smashing and burning my drums,
cutting off my hands, and silencing my tongue
had only known that *my story* was in her essence,
housed by her womb,
hidden away in her sacred walls,
what atrocity would they have attempted to quiet her?

I thank the One Omnipotent God
for giving her infinite strength and endurance,
for the foresight needed to safeguard *our story.*
She is the embodiment of the song of a griot, jali,
my past, present, and my future.
I pray that she forever
tells my story!

10. POE 44

[In the voice of Edgar Allen Poe]

Once upon a midnight weary
they heard his last name
and chose to fear, see.
Quill in hand
as Poe heard the criticism of Obama.
His citizenship questioned,
not one-hundred percent black
due to the ancestry of his momma.

How would Poe address
the "nays" and the "yays"?
What editorial would he use
to describe Obama's 2,920 days?

With a magnifying glass in hand,
thou seek to find his unpatriotic ways.

Only to discover his political lore.
Thou criticized with scrutiny
like no other white man before,
he who is but one amongst 44.

More than two hundred and forty years of lies,
corruption, oppression, and wars.
Expecting his pen to correct all errs,
to right all wrongs
which would realistically
take at least forty more.
A proud lady on his arm
that is respected by most.
Held in high regard with a presidential toast.
Though some may pass judgment on their efforts
amongst the poor.
He who is but one amongst 44

Darryl A. Lewis

The first Black to hold the position
which may be up for debate.
There's possibly a Black Moor
that we've discovered of late.
But from slavery since emancipation,
he's opened a black door,
he who is but one amongst 44.

Whether he was an adulterer
equal to the Kennedys
who was loved by many;
whether he lied like Nixon
whose lies were plenty.

Even if he had flooded
the streets with drugs like Reagan.
Faked weapons of mass destruction.
Called Black people super predators
pied pipered saxophones and cigars
were his preferred tools of seduction.

One thing we cannot debate,
and most won't deny.
He's not the first politician to ever tell a lie.
Cherry trees are strange fables gone awry.
Like that orange coif in the wind
on top of the head of 45.

Obama, towards the end
grey hairs, were more than before.
The future only knows
if he'll be hated or one that we adore,
if his jump shot at the buzzer
will be considered a score.
But one thing is a fact,
he was but one amongst 44.

11. TEARS

Have you ever heard a black man cry?
Sounds like the squeal
of a baby seal being clubbed.
Such a gut-wrenching sound.
Grown-ass man crying.

Crying out of frustration.
Kidnapped on an ice land.
Forced to wear the clothing of a beast.
Never seen as a man.
Listed on the manifest as chattel,
herded through a forest.

Forest of oak trees.
Trees transformed into weeping willows.
Black woman sleeping next to tear-stained, empty
pillow.

Pillow-soft body.
Now black woman
must be strong.
She has his seed to harvest.

Harvest is sharecropped.
They handpick a chosen few.
Boule' bully black man too.
Monetize his melanin.
Repackage it and sell it again and again and again.
Strip him of his birthright.
False sense of identity turned Anthony Johnson white.
Where'd all his land go?
Oh, he still ain't white though.

Darryl A. Lewis

Though a black man cries,
his tear drops are balled-up fists.
Black man cries Jack Johnson, Joe Louis, Mike Tyson
hard.
They hear him.
Fear him.
Find him.
Club him.
Pose for the camera.
Wear his pelt.

Have you ever heard a black man cry,
writhing in pain?
He can't breathe!
Sounds like the squeal
of a baby seal being clubbed.
Such a gut-wrenching sound.
Grown-ass man crying.

CHAPTER THREE
LORD

1. CATTLE ON A THOUSAND HILLS

Verse 1:

Sometimes it seems like there is no way out
I'm overwhelmed by circumstance
My heart is filled with doubt
The Word tells me, there's a master plan
I open up my heart and I'm guided by His hand

Chorus:

I've got cattle, on a thousand hills
Cattle on a thousand hills
I've got cattle, on a thousand hills
Cattle on a thousand hills
I've got cattle, on a thousand hills
Cattle on a thousand hills
I've got cattle, on a thousand hills
Cattle on a thousand hills

Verse 2:

I'm my father's child, not born to be without
Every step, I take in faith, no longer move in doubt
The Word, it tells me, I never move alone
If I should ask for bread, He'll never give me stone

Chorus:

Change:

I've got cattle on a hill
I've got more than a thousand cattle
I've got cattle on a hill
I've got more than a thousand cattle
Chorus: (Modulate) [Vamp Out]

2. THE FORMULA

Verse 1:

Cigarette blunt, bong, or bowl
Took a hit of that "Je"
That "sus"(tains) my soul...
Cigarette blunt, bong, or bowl
Took a hit of that "Je"
That "sus"(tains) my soul...
Held dat spirit in my lungs
Until I coughed up my pain
Fell down on my knees
My life will never be the same

Who knew, I had to experience the light
In order to know that I was blind?
Who knew, that once I saw the light
the beauty I would find?
Who knew, once I could see
I'd find the heaven in me?
Who knew I had unlimited potential?
Who knew I had infinite possibilities?
Who knew I could move mountains?
With the faith of a mustard seed?
The formula...

Chorus:

Love God, have faith in my vision and forgive
Love God, have faith in my vision and forgive
Love God, have faith in my vision and forgive
What'chu know about dat?
Reborn, rebirthed, a spiritual revelation revolution
No longer a prisoner, of this physical plain institution

Verse 2:

I don't Crip Walk but
But I "Christ talk," whoopty-whoop, in His steps
Blood drenched, fist clenched, still swinging till that
last breath
I'm not concerned with a color
I'm concerned with son, daughter, of a mother
I pay my respect as Jesus wept

I'm not perfect
Perfection is not a destination
But a journey that never ends
A never-ending, winding yellow-brick road
that twists and turns
Flying monkeys continuously hurling feces at me
As I try to find my way home back to

"Auntie Em, Auntie Em"

If you thought you'd reached perfection
you need to remove that veil of arrogance
from your eyes
and read the sign again

You've dozed off and missed your stop: reality
Best to get off before the last stop: mortality
Riding on a train called humanity
Driven by a conductor called insanity
Thought you were in a land called Democracy
Realized you were in a capitalist hell called Hypocrisy

You can pick up your baggage, or leave it, move fast or
move slow
I am forgiven, and I forgive
I've already been all the wrong ways
There's only one way left to go

Chorus:

Love God, have faith in my vision and forgive
Love God, have faith in my vision and forgive
Love God, have faith in my vision and forgive
What'chu know about dat?
Reborn, rebirthed, a spiritual revelation revolution
No longer a prisoner, of this physical plain institution

Verse 3:

Don't fault me for bleeding
on society's white shag rug
Fault them for stabbing me in the chest, with hate
greed, and jealousy
And stepping back to mean-mug

You purchased me, caged me, raped me, castrated me,
bred me to be strong, to fight
Then, sit back amongst yourselves, eating southern
biscuits, drinking sweet tea
Trying to figure out, why do I bite?

Self-preservation, isn't that my God-given right?

For every crack
that was heard from the sound of your whip
it's only natural to wish, I could return the favor with
the crack, of my pistol grip

Fast forward to now

They tricked me
into aiming a barrel at my own mirror
How was I so frustrated with hate
that I attempted to kill my own reflection?

That's not him; that's me!
That's my mother dressed in black
tears streaming down her face
on the verge of collapse
Her wig shifted to the left, revealing her nylon cap
Eyes piercing the heavens to make eye contact ... with
God Himself
On her knees, to ask him, "Why, why?"

That's my family
gathered around her to console her
to reiterate that I was too young to die
How did I become their appendage
perpetrating my own genocide, for a facade called
wealth?
I guess someday I'll have to forgive myself

Chorus:

Love God, have faith in my vision and forgive
Love God, have faith in my vision and forgive
Love God, have faith in my vision and forgive

What'chu know about dat?
Reborn, rebirthed, a spiritual revelation revolution
No longer a prisoner, of this physical plain institution

3. I CAN'T COMPLAIN
Key of G Major

Verse 1

You called my mother home and said it's time to rest
In Your divine embrace, I know she's blessed
Strength and faith, Your love's what she possessed
And I appreciate, (pause), just how You blessed me

She was Your vessel, to lay hands on me
I took it for granted then, but now I can see
Though I long, to touch her face
In my heart's her special place; You blessed me

Chorus

I can't complain
No, I can't complain
I can't complain
No, I can't complain
I know I forget sometimes
I guess it just slips my mind
The Comforter whispers,
"It will all work out fine."
Because You bless me

Verse 2

If I close my eyes, I can still see her face
Her words are so clear, time could never erase
Thoughts of her, fill my empty space
I appreciate, (pause) how You blessed me
Years come and go; tears come and go
But she'll always be with me
that's one thing I know

This flesh is only here for the moment
the spirit's forever
I know we'll be together
'cause You blessed me

Chorus

I can't complain
No, I can't complain
I can't complain
No, I can't complain
I know I forget sometimes
I guess it just slips my mind
The Comforter whispers,
"It will all work out fine."

Bridge

Sometimes loneliness seems too hard to bear
I'm reassured when I see her footsteps everywhere!
I realized that the fight she fought was won
When You took her hand and said, "My child, well done!"

Chorus

Half-Step up a key

I can't complain
No, I can't complain
I can't complain
No, I can't complain
I know I forget sometimes
I guess it just slips my mind
The Comforter whispers,
"It will all work out fine."

Half-Step up a key

I can't complain
No, I can't complain
I can't complain

Damn the Pain (Love, Life, and Lord)

No, I can't complain
I know I forget sometimes
I guess it just slips my mind
The Comforter whispers,
"It will all work out fine."
Because You bless me

4. SOMEBODY NEEDS TO TELL SOMEBODY

Intro-(Rapped)

I'm lyrically superior
I'm making the devil wearier
I'm putting the God of fear in you
And look at your eyes get tearier, as you stare
Wondering how a brother got there!
Spitting those Holy-Ghost lyrics
without a worry or a care
I'm the type of brother that you feed about
Holy-Ghost filled, tripped up, and then you read about
Picked myself up, shook it off, and now you know
Thanks to the Word, my soul is whiter than snow

Verse 1

I'd searched from the mountains
to the valleys so low
and had yet to find the answer
for true contentment in my soul

While my Father tried to tell me
my indiscretions covered my ears
It's time to look to the heavens
The Bible tells you if your heart will hear!

Chorus – (Choir)

Somebody needs to tell somebody 'bout Jesus
Somebody needs to tell somebody 'bout my Lord
Somebody needs to tell it!
Somebody needs to tell. Go tell it, won'tcha?
Somebody needs to tell somebody 'bout my Lord

Verse 2

To feed of the things of this world
will not satisfy my soul

'Cause one day the two of us must part
Like a fool and his gold

And I believe that to believe in the Word
Of Jehovah will help to get me through
He's, my shepherd; I shall not want
And John 1:14 will tell you who!

Chorus - (Choir)

Change - (Choir—Women Only)

Jesus is the answer; love is the way
To gravitate from the trials and tribulations of today
He is the key
He died for you, and He also died for me
Let Him lift you up
It's for all mankind to share His loving cup
Trying to find a way?
Get down on your knees, my people, and pray.

Change 2

Calling my brother
And calling out to my sisters too
If you're lost, just **cry out** (cry out) and the Shepherd will
find you

Vamp Out

(Somebody, Somebody, Somebody, Somebody) *Repeat*
(Somebody needs to tell it. Somebody needs to tell. Go
tell it, won'tcha?)
Gone tell 'em with my word (2X)
(Somebody needs to tell it. Somebody needs to tell. Go
tell it, won'tcha?) *Repeat*
Gone tell 'em by the things I do
Right now, I'm talking about me!
But, what about you and you and you?
(Get down on your knees!)
Gone tell 'em with my mouth

Darryl A. Lewis

Gone tell 'em with my hands
(Get down on your knees!)
Gone tell 'em with my feet
(He is the key!)
Gone tell every "who" I meet!
(He is the key!)
(Get down on your knees, my people, and pray...)
[Explosion]

5. TOO BUSY THINKING ABOUT MY BLESSINGS
(Remix of "Too Busy Thinking About My Baby" by Marvin Gaye)

Verse 1

I ain't got time
To wake up and wonder
Who's talking bad about me
And I ain't got time
To criticize and judge
Somebody's sexuality

Verse 2

And I don't have the time
To think about, The New York Stock Exchange
And I never give it a second thought
Why today it had to rain

Chorus

Too busy thinking about my blessings
And I ain't got time for nothing else
Too busy thinking about my blessings
And I ain't got time for nothing else

Verse 3

I ain't got time to discuss the recession
Or how long it's gonna last
I ain't got time to study war no more
The rising price of gas

Bridge 1

Telling you I'm, just a person
I got, love and gratitude on my mind
When it comes to
Thinking about anything but, my blessings

I just don't have the time

Chorus

Verse 4

All the silver and gold
Could never satisfy my soul
Please...! I got inspiration, revelation
People tell you
I got heaven right here on Earth!

Bridge 1

You see, I'm, just a person
I got, love and gratitude on my mind
When it comes to
Thinking about anything but, my blessings
I just don't have the time

Chorus

(Vamp Out)

6. I GOT JESUS ON MY MIND

Verse 1

Woke up this morning with love on my heart
Hate tries to visit but it soon departs
John 1:14 said the Word became flesh
Ran through the valley, and He passed the test

Chorus 1

I got Jesus; I got Jesus on my mind
I got Jesus; I got Jesus on my mind
Rising above, I'm propelled by love
'Cause I got Jesus on my mind

Verse 2

I see the trials and I feel the pain
But my joy's within and my peace remains
I feel the wet when the rain does fall
But my soul is confident; He's conquered all

Chorus 1

I got Jesus; I got Jesus on my mind
I got Jesus; I got Jesus on my mind
Rising above, I'm propelled by love
'Cause I got Jesus on my mind

Verse 3

When I lay me, down to sleep
I pray the Lord my, soul to keep
If I should cross over before I wake
I'm heaven bound, for Jesus' sake!

Chorus 2

I got Jesus; I got Jesus on my mind
I got Jesus; I got Jesus on my mind

You might see me dancing in the middle of the day
'Cause I got Jesus on my mind

Outro

I see your weapons, but they cannot win
He's in my being; He's more than just my friend
'Cause, He's love, and I got it!
He's peace, and I got it!
He's joy, and I got it!

7. I GOT JESUS ON MY MIND (PT. 2)

(Sing)

I got Jesus; I got Jesus on my mind.
I got Jesus; I got Jesus on my mind.
Rising above, I'm propelled by love,
'Cause I got Jesus on my mind.

I got Jesus on my mind.
No, not you:
Mr. Preacher,
Mr. Evangelist,
Mr. Missionary,
Mr. Brother Prophet or Ms. Sister Prophetess,
Mr. Priest or Miss Priestess,
Not even you, Mr. Pope,
Nope!

Jesus, the physical manifestation of the Word of God!
In accordance with the word
that you feed your flock so sparingly.
The Word that became flesh
and made His dwelling among us.

In one breath you tell me that man
cannot live by bread alone
and then turn around
and give me a biscuit without the two piece,
give me the bun without the beef.
You eat the meat and leave me the bone.
Now gone, with that!

I got Jesus on my mind.
Not your reiteration
of the interpretation of the versions
that the different authorities be spurting
as if they have the only direct true line to God.
Naysayers constantly spewing out their aspersions.

Darryl A. Lewis

To cut through the rhetoric,
you almost have to be a master surgeon—

Let's just say you have to be very open-minded
to marry your word.
It's been touched by a lot of men
far from a virgin.

Rumors going around,
people talking about what they heard and
sometimes spliced and laid out,
filling communion glasses with Thunderbird.

To oppress or control.
To put fear in my heart.
and then pretend to console.
Charlatans collecting payments
for mansions of gold,
in heaven?

They strike out like venomous snakes
for whom the bell tolls.

Doing all that dirt in Jesus' name.
People like that should burn in a special part of hell,
by a special type of flame.

How dare they cloak their lies in Jesus.
When truly what they despise is Jesus.
Contradictory to everything in their life is Jesus.
They should be happy
that there is no more "eye for an eye,"

thanks to Jesus!

8. BROWN CHURCH STEEPLE

I see you, brown church steeple
pointing into the grey clouds
like a large concrete finger, but I am confused.

Are you showing me
a perplexed being in the sky,
who's pondering
the hypocrisy of the people inside?

While outside
there's a homeless man
with his back against the wall
sitting on your cold church steps,
holding out a rusty tin can
with "God Bless You"
written in red magic marker
on a piece of cardboard,
taped on that rusty tin can,
a few feet below a black sign
with large white letters
 that say, "I AM."

That homeless man is sporadically
talking out loud to no one walking past him.
Is he praying?

Darryl A. Lewis

I see you, brown church steeple
pointing into the grey clouds
like a large concrete finger
as its hand pulls the chord
that rings a brass bell in the air
to announce that it's suppertime,
to gather God's children.

I see you up there,
you have my attention,
but when the vibrations
from the clang of the bell stops
and everyone arrives to holds hands,
sing songs, do penance, be spiritually fed,
cry on each other's shoulders,
lift their heads to the heavens
and shout
"Hallelujah!"
will it make a difference
to that homeless man
with his back against the wall
sitting on your cold church steps?
I'm just wondering,
brown church steeple.

9. FORBIDDEN FRUIT

I know the forbidden fruit.
I know why it is there
in the garden for all to see.

I know there is no redemption
without temptation.

I realize
I am unable to walk
through the doors of heaven
if I am not able to deny myself.

I know why it seems more beautiful
than any other fruit in the garden,
but I dare not taste.

Its colors are infinite
there has never been an enticement more vibrant.

Its shapes are boundless
though there has never been another shape
more appealing to the human eye.

The aromas are sweet, and variants are vast,
yet I could never fill my nostrils to satisfaction.

I no longer wander,
lost in the forest of my own ignorance.
The Forbidden Fruit just lies there,
seductress, in the middle of the garden.

10. GOD MUST BE MISERABLE

If there's a God of love and compassion,
why doesn't He see me here
sitting in this church doorway
dressed in four layers of clothes?
I am my only closet.
My skin and hair only see water when it rains.
Can He smell me?

Passers-by all seem to smell me.
I watch them hold their noses
and frown when I ask them for the spare change,
the coins that they would eventually lose
in the cushions of their sofas.

Does God look past me
like His so-called Christians
in fine clothes look past me?

They judge me.
When by the grace of God
our roles could have been switched.
They don't know my story.

Is God deaf or
did He choose not
to hear my screams as a child?
Was He too busy to at least check on me?
Was that why He put me on this planet,
to have my innocence beat and stripped away?
Was this my God-given purpose?
Images still haunt me on the daily.
Voices come out of my head,
holding invasive conversations with me!
I yell now with words
I should have said back then.

I try to drown the screams

with whatever intoxicant or drug
that I can get my hands on,
but they still seep through like a caustic acid
and dissolve any hopes I might have had.

Nietzsche proclaimed God was dead
just before he died from syphilis.

Is the sight of me so pathetic?

Is my image too much to bear?
Is that why people look away?
Someone said I was made in God's image.
That would mean
His face is just as ugly as mine.

Maybe ladies with pretty dresses
and red-bottom shoes
walk past him
while holding scented white handkerchiefs
over their noses too.

What stops God
from at least dropping coins in my cup?
With all the money He gets
from His big fancy buildings!

He can't even take the time
to be sure that one of His beloved "children"
is properly fed and has a place to sleep?

The man across the street
with the microphone and the speakers
and the "Jesus Loves You" sign
yelled out, "Jesus loves you, Brother!"
He says, God is in me too.

I find that hard to believe
when my stomach is caving in

and I barely have enough energy to look up!

Can't God see that I'm hungry?
Couldn't He be sure that I at least
find a half-eaten sandwich when I rummage
through the garbage cans?

I hurt so bad!

I scream His name to the top of my lungs
"GOD!"

curled up
next to a dumpster in the alley.
The only answer to my prayers
is smell of piss and garbage,
the scurrying of cat and rat paws
hitting against the concrete.

If God is in me,
He must be miserable!

Acknowledgments

I'd like to give thanks to the One Omnipotent God for the spiritual and conscious journey and influences He has gifted me. I am so thankful for each stop I've made and that has become a part of my spiritual construct. I thank my sister Danielle Lewis for her ride-or-die mentality. To my children Berét DeWeese, Darryl Jr, Darrian, and last but not least, Darriella, for listening to all my ideas and giving me her opinions (even when I don't ask for them), reciting my poems along with me to let me know how many times she has heard them. All my family and friends in Charlotte, N.C, too many to name. I can't thank Felicia Cade enough for being a constant sounding board for my ideas and her **Power of Words (P.O.W.):** Jim Ruggirello, **HomeLand Cultural Center, Long Beach, CA,** for reigniting my creative flame and drawing me back into the creative community and having faith to hire me to perform at their events. Orlando Greenhill and Sound Army for introducing me to freedom of expression and all my O.G. Skittles: Solar Vexus, Tony Silva, Alex Villeda, Jesus Miguel Serna, Joseph Stowers, Ricky Wood, Ryan Banks, Be Marz for shocking me into appreciating their form of expression and inspiring me to think outside the box and unleashing my inner "Bad Brains."

Cultural Alliance of Long Beach: Keith Lilly, Victor Ladd

Baba Olufemi Viltz, Baba Raymond (Yaya) Quarles, Baba John Beattie, Baba Hanif, Mama Ndella Davis-Diassy, Crystal James for introducing me to, and sharing with me, the beauty of the African culture in spirituality, drum, and dance. I was so blessed to be able to share this with my children.

Adonna Kenlow, Carl Johnson, Linda Iverson, Dennis Pearson, Linda Delmar, Karyse Payne, Ashlee Davis, Tabitha VI Christopher, Molimau Andrew Fatu, Lance Lowe, Samuel Rain, Jeremiah White, Charlie E. Scott III, Brina "Melanin Princess" Clark, Micheaux Fortson (UrbanVoodoo), Mike Rivera.

Shades of Africa: Renee Quarles, Isaac Sundiata, Shy But Flyy, Pacc Crowell, James Stewart, Savvy Raw, Linda Bolongo, El Fickling, Kevin Land, Simi Blair, Anfaani Henry.

Darryl A. Lewis

Still Waters Writers Group: Oshea & Melanie Luja opened the door to the spoken-word community even wider for me. Baridi Kipande Cha Kazi (A Kold Piece), Taalam Acey, Donny Jackson,
Kuahmel Allah, Eternal Mind, Kiyatana Sapp, Jessica Gallion, LaLa DeVille, Ric-Roc, Renee Chatman, Derek D. Brown, Tommy Domino, Sipho N'Jedi T'Challa, Mars Gambino, Kershawn Ware, Marcellus, William TheEnova, Mark Antonius Junius, Artus Mansoir, Korlah Collins, Ieshya Parker, Janaci, Vickie (Ms. Vickie) Hurt, Sabreen Shabazz, Zanetta Tribble.
World Stage: Ms. Venela "V. Kali" Flagg, Conney Williams, Jaha Zainabu, **Hillard Street,**
S. Pearl Sharp, Kamau Daaood, Peter J. Harris, Jawanza Dumisani, Nadia Hunter Bey,
River GahMatah Oshun, Michelle Williams, Michael Datcher, Heather Parker,
Hiram Charles Sims, Rob "Poetry" Morrow, Tasha Auset Ahsat.
SWAAM: Lorenzo Frank, Dennis DeLoach
Donald Reed, Donaldo "Bluesman" Reed, thank you for giving me an outlet to sing my Spanish songs. Ann Van Wellman, Mary Tawadros. Charlene E. Green for her assistance in editing.

To think that this is but a portion of the people I have laughed with, workshopped with, performed with, cried with, and who have contributed to these pieces in one way or another. Please forgive me if I didn't note you here, but I didn't want the Acknowledgments to be longer than the book! I do appreciate you!